Caitlin Clark

Basketball Superstar and Inspiration for a New Generation

Leanne Currie-McGhee

San Diego, CA

About the Author

Leanne Currie-McGhee has written books for the past two decades. She lives in Norfolk, Virginia, with her husband, Keith, daughters, Grace and Sol, and their dog, Delilah.

© 2025 ReferencePoint Press, Inc.
Printed in the United States

For more information, contact:
ReferencePoint Press, Inc.
PO Box 27779
San Diego, CA 92198
www.ReferencePointPress.com

ALL RIGHTS RESERVED.
No part of this work covered by the copyright hereon may be reproduced or used in any form or by any means—graphic, electronic, or mechanical, including photocopying, recording, taping, web distribution, or information storage retrieval systems—without the written permission of the publisher.

Picture Credits:
Cover: Brian Rothmuller/Icon Sportswire DHZ/ Brian Rothmuller/Icon Sportswire/Newscom
6: Associated Press
10: © Steven Garcia/ZUMA Press Wire/Alamy Stock Photo
13: Associated Press
17: Associated Press
19: Marc Piscotty/Icon Sportswire 141/Marc Piscotty/Icon Sportswire/Newscom
22: Sipa USA/Alamy Live News
27: Associated Press
30: Associated Press
33: Associated Press
37: Associated Press
40: Keith Gillett/Icon Sportswire CFP/Keith Gillett/Icon Sportswire/Newscom
42: Associated Press
47: Associated Press
51: Sports Press Photo/Shaina Benhiyoun/SPP/Sipa USA/Newscom
53: Associated Press

LIBRARY OF CONGRESS CATALOGING-IN-PUBLICATION DATA

Names: Currie-McGhee, Leanne, 1971- author.
Title: Caitlin Clark : basketball superstar and inspiration for a new generation / by Leanne Currie-McGhee.
Description: San Diego, CA : ReferencePoint Press, Inc., 2025. | Includes bibliographical references and index. | Audience term: Teenagers
Identifiers: LCCN 2024044857 (print) | LCCN 2024044858 (ebook) | ISBN 9781678210007 (library binding) | ISBN 9781678210014 (ebook)
Subjects: LCSH: Clark, Caitlin, 2002---Juvenile literature. | Basketball players--United States--Biography--Juvenile literature. | Women basketball players--United States--Biography--Juvenile literature.
Classification: LCC GV884.C554 C87 2024 (print) | LCC GV884.C554 (ebook) | DDC 796.323092 [B]--dc23/eng/20240927
LC record available at https://lccn.loc.gov/2024044857
LC ebook record available at https://lccn.loc.gov/2024044858

CONTENTS

Introduction   **4**
Finding Her Path

Chapter One   **8**
Early Years

Chapter Two   **16**
High School Stardom

Chapter Three   **25**
Transition to College Basketball

Chapter Four   **36**
Rising to National Prominence

Chapter Five   **46**
Going Pro

Source Notes   56
Important Events in the Life of Caitlin Clark   59
For Further Research   61
Index   63

INTRODUCTION

Finding Her Path

Caitlin Clark's basketball talent was evident when she was just five years old. But that alone does not explain how she became a professional athlete. Her determination, fearlessness, fierce competitiveness, and at times even her impatience, have all contributed to her journey from talented player to elite athlete. That journey has been marked by a series of bold choices, great confidence, and a passion for the sport of basketball.

Playing with the Boys

As a kid, Clark often played soccer, basketball, and football with her brothers. She picked up any sport easily. However, her basketball ability and love for the game always made it her top sport. From the moment Clark first picked up a basketball, her quick reflexes, sharp shooting, and court vision set her apart from her peers.

Her talent led to frustration and impatience with those who could not keep up with her level of play. In the case of basketball, when she was young there were not local girls' teams that were competitive enough to challenge her. And as competitive as she was, her parents knew she needed a challenge to keep her interested. That is what led her father to enroll her on a boys' club basketball team.

Clark's father scoured the area for a competitive environment that would allow her to grow and develop her skills. When he couldn't find a girls' team on her level, he found a boys' team that was a good fit. She was still in elementary school when he signed her up for that team—and agreed to be its coach.

Early Success

Not everyone was thrilled with Clark's presence on the boys' team. But the issue was not that they thought a girl couldn't keep up with the boys. Clark was one of the leading players. Clark's father remembers a mother complaining because she was not comfortable with a girl outperforming her sons. However, these criticisms were ignored by Clark, her family, and the team.

Clark primarily played as a point guard, a position with the responsibility of advancing the basketball up the court and setting up the team's offense. This position requires a combination of agility, intelligence, and shooting prowess. Clark excelled in this role, showcasing her ability to read the game and make plays needed for the team to score. When Clark was in second grade, the team went on to win a state championship, and her talent contributed to the team's success.

Unwavering Support

Clark often credits her parents for their open-minded approach to letting her push hard in basketball and other areas of her life. "My parents never told me not to do something because I was a girl,"[1] she recalls. In addition to that, her brothers pushed her to play as hard as possible. When they played with her, they did not hold back. This supportive environment allowed Clark to pursue her dreams without the constraints of traditional gender roles. She learned to focus on her competitiveness and drive to excel.

> "My parents never told me not to do something because I was a girl."[1]
>
> —Caitlin Clark

With the family behind her, Clark continued to play basketball with boys until the sixth grade. At that point, her parents found a competitive girls' team. The players were older than Clark, which gave her more of a challenge. Having played with the boys for so long helped push her limits, and she learned to excel in a challenging environment. It toughened her up, honed her skills, and taught her to compete at a high level. Many of those boys—former teammates and boys from other teams—are now her biggest fans, proud to have shared the court with her during those formative years.

Knowing Her Goals

Clark knew what she wanted as a kid. At nine years old, she knew what she wanted to achieve and had no doubts that she would do so. In third grade she wrote a list of her goals as part of a class assignment. Two of the most ambitious dreams on that list were to get a basketball scholarship to play in college, and eventually

Caitlin Clark's childhood dream was to play professionally with the Women's National Basketball Association. She achieved that goal in 2024 when she was drafted number one by the Indiana Fever.

play professionally with the Women's National Basketball Association (WNBA), the US women's professional league, which was established in 1997.

Her mom, Anne Nizzi-Clark, still has that list. It reminds everyone of Clark's dreams and how focused she was on achieving them. "It's pretty special, looking back at that sheet I was able to check off a lot of goals,"[2] Clark said as she showed it during the WNBA draft of 2024.

The list turned out to be a road map for her future. Her journey to breaking the National Collegiate Athletic Association (NCAA) women's all-time scoring record while at the University of Iowa, creating the "Caitlin effect" of increasing popularity for women's basketball, and being the 2024 WNBA number one draft started with that list. Her story shows that dreams can turn into reality with hard work and dedication.

CHAPTER ONE

Early Years

Family, faith, and sports were the main focus of Caitlin Clark's childhood. Clark, called Caitie by her family when she was a child, was born in West Des Moines, Iowa, on January 22, 2002. She grew up in a close-knit family environment that played a significant role in shaping her life and her athletic journey. Her parents, siblings, grandparents, and cousins created a strong sense of togetherness and community in Clark's life and laid the groundwork for her developing self-confidence.

A Sporty Family

Athletics have been an integral part of Clark's family life. Her father, Brent Clark, played baseball and basketball in college and later coached youth basketball teams. Her older brother, Blake, played football for Iowa State, and as of 2024, her younger brother, Colin, was playing high school basketball. Her grandfather, Bob Nizzi, was a high school football coach.

With a father and grandfather who coached, and siblings and cousins who played sports, athletics has always been central to Clark's life. In addition to playing, her family often watched sports and attended games together. "We were always involved in sports and at home we were always around sports," her brother Blake says. "We watched sports at night whether we would go to Drake [a university in Iowa] and watch basketball games, or watch cousins play their basketball games, or tournaments, when you're just around something that much, it's what you do, too."[3] And Clark recalls that women's basketball games were among the games they watched.

> "We were always involved in sports and at home we were always around sports."[3]
>
> —Blake Clark, Caitlin Clark's brother

In fact, sports were very important in her and her brothers' lives—and her parents used that fact when disciplining their kids. Clark recalls that in sixth or seventh grade, she came home from school and got into a heated argument with her brothers. While she does not remember what the argument was about, she does remember the consequence. None of the kids were allowed to go to the high school girls' basketball game that night.

Clark frequently played games, typically basketball, with her brothers and cousins. These family games were more than just casual play. They were intense, competitive, and physically demanding. Clark often found herself playing basketball with Blake and his friends—and she got no special treatment because she was younger or a girl. This experience was pivotal in developing her toughness and competitive edge. "My older brother was just bigger, stronger, faster,"[4] Caitlin recalls, highlighting how playing with him pushed her to improve and compete at a higher level.

Clark was not limited to just one sport. From a young age, she excelled in soccer, softball, tennis, volleyball, and basketball. This broad exposure to various sports helped her develop a well-rounded athletic skill set, contributing to her abilities on the basketball court.

Competitive Spirit

While sports were a major part of her everyday life, another was her family's faith. Raised in a Catholic household, her faith played a significant role in her upbringing. She and her family were active participants at their parish and attended church regularly. She also attended Catholic schools through twelfth grade.

Sports were not the only activity that routinely brought Clark's family together. They often ate dinner together and gathered for holidays. Other activities included baking with their mother and the three kids playing video games together.

Even video game nights were competitive. Clark's competitive spirit was a defining feature of her personality growing up,

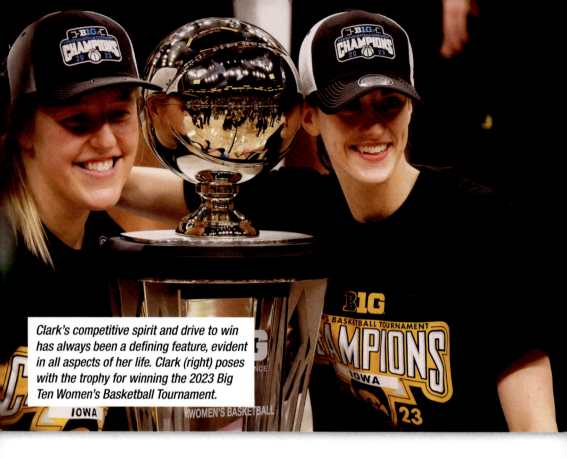

Clark's competitive spirit and drive to win has always been a defining feature, evident in all aspects of her life. Clark (right) poses with the trophy for winning the 2023 Big Ten Women's Basketball Tournament.

evident in all aspects of her life. She had an intense desire to win, whether it was in sports or board games. "Very competitive. She was always very, very smart," one of Clark's former teachers said in an interview. "The passion and the drive. The tenacity that you see on the court, you could see on the playground."[5]

Early on, Clark says, her drive to win led to instances when she became too intense. Clark sometimes became upset when other players could not keep up with her style of play. "She got a little frustrated because she was talented, so she had to play up a couple of years," Brent Clark says of her time playing softball. "And even then . . . playing shortstop [in softball], the girls would have a hard time catching her throws."[6]

Sometimes, her frustration surfaced. Clark recalls how her parents received calls from the elementary school to let them know that their daughter was getting angry and frustrated when she lost a game in PE class. At other times, her competitive drive led to emotional reactions, such as crying when she was having a hard time during a basketball game. According to Clark's grandfather, Bob Nizzi, when this happened on her club basketball team, her coach-father would pull her out of the game. He would tell her to sit on the bench, giving her time to refocus her energy and learn to deal with her intense emotions. As time went by, she learned to put that intensity into her play.

> "She got a little frustrated because she was talented, so she had to play up a couple of years."[6]
>
> —Brent Clark, Caitlin Clark's father

Finding a Team

By the time his daughter had reached sixth grade, Brent Clark realized that she needed greater competition in basketball. He found a girls' team with the challenging environment she needed to stay engaged and motivated. Caitlin Clark joined the All Iowa Attack, a girls' basketball league known for its high level of competition and emphasis on player development. The team was part of the Amateur Athletic Union, a group that runs amateur sports programs worldwide. Her teammates were a year older than she was. This environment was exactly what Clark needed.

She thrived, honing her skills and competing against some of the best young talents in the region. The All Iowa Attack

Overheated Play

Caitlin Clark is the first to admit that her passion for winning sometimes got the best of her when she was young. She recalls one snow day when she and her brothers had a day off from school. They were playing a Nerf basketball game in the basement. Sometimes their games got quite heated. Colin was defending against his sister and caused her to miss a shot. Caitlin got so mad she pushed her brother toward the wall. "I was just getting so angry . . . that I just chucked [Colin] into the wall. And he put his hand back [behind his head] . . . and there was just blood everywhere," Caitlin recalls. Off to the hospital he and his mom went, and doctors used staples to close the cut. Colin recovered and their games continued, but the incident was a reminder of just how fiercely competitive Caitlin could be, even at a young age.

Quoted in Heavy, "Brothers 'Were Just Awful' to Caitlin Clark Growing Up: Mom," Heavy.com, 2024. https://heavy.com.

program director and coach of Clark's team, Dickson Jensen, immediately recognized Clark's talent and saw that she had a work ethic to match. Clark rose up through the club ranks quickly. Playing with and against older, talented girls pushed her to improve. The All Iowa Attack league played a significant role in her development, helping her build the competitive edge and advanced skills that would later define her high school and college basketball career.

Getting Noticed

Clark's extraordinary talent in basketball started attracting attention from Division I college coaches even before she reached high school. Her standout play with the All Iowa Attack team was drawing notice. Coaches from prestigious college programs began making calls to inquire about her. This early interest was unusual, highlighting just how exceptional Clark's abilities were.

The coaches and scouts who watched Clark play were immediately struck by her basketball skills and her understanding of the sport. Jan Jensen, University of Iowa associate head coach and chief recruiter, had heard of Clark when she was in sixth grade. Not long after, Jensen watched Clark sink her signature deep three-pointers (shots from a specific range that are worth three, as opposed to the typical two, points) and knew she wanted Clark on the Iowa Hawkeyes team. "It didn't take but a second, maybe a minute," Jensen recounts. "That little step-back sassy 3 [-point shot], this little seventh, eighth grader. Yeah, she's diff. You could just tell. They're easy to identify, but really hard to get. Everybody can see the true, true ones. The trick is to get them."[7] Although it would be several years until Clark graduated from high school, Jensen already knew she wanted Clark on her team.

> "That little step-back sassy 3 [basketball move], this little seventh, eighth grader. Yeah, she's diff. You could just tell."[7]
>
> —Jan Jensen, University of Iowa associate head coach and chief recruiter

It was not just her signature moves, like the step-back three, that showcased Clark's technical skills. Jenson noticed she was a confi-

Jan Jensen, University of Iowa associate head coach and chief recruiter, had heard of Clark when she was in the sixth grade. Jensen scouted Clark early on and knew she wanted her on the Iowa Hawkeyes' team.

dent player who made precise passes that were often too much for her teammates to handle and that Clark was creative on her drives to score. Her ability to execute and develop complex plays at such a young age was a clear indication of her advanced skill level and potential. These attributes made her a prime target for college recruiters who could see her potential to excel at the next level.

Parents Keeping Check

Despite the growing attention and early recruitment efforts, Clark's parents were determined to ensure she had a normal childhood. They managed the influx of interested calls from colleges, regulating both calls and interactions to prevent her from becoming overwhelmed. This approach allowed their daughter to focus on her development and enjoy being a kid without the added pressure of constant recruitment.

Her parents' efforts to shield her from the overwhelming attention paid off. Clark was able to enjoy her time in middle school and

Girl Inspiration

Caitlin Clark's love of basketball was partly inspired by watching her older girl cousins. Clark idolized her two cousins, Haley and Audrey Faber, because they starred on the Dowling Catholic High School girls' basketball team. Clark vividly remembers going to see them play as a kid on Tuesday and Friday nights during the basketball season. Her cousins even let her come along with them to team dinners. Clark saw them continue to follow a path with basketball after they graduated, showing her that basketball could be a part of her future. Haley Faber went on to become part of the Iowa State University basketball staff. Audrey Faber, who played at Nebraska's Creighton University, later became an assistant coach at Dowling. Clark also remembers traveling an hour and a half in the car to see Audrey Faber's games at Creighton. Seeing her cousins play motivated Clark to push even harder in her own basketball career, knowing she could make her own future with basketball at the center.

focus on honing her skills without the constant distraction of college scouts. She also kept her focus on academics and other activities. Clark played other sports, such as softball and soccer, and even took piano lessons. This balance was crucial in maintaining her love for the game and preventing burnout at a young age.

Dickson Jensen highlighted the role Clark's parents played in keeping her grounded. They were appreciative of the opportunities that their daughter received but remained mindful of the importance of maintaining humility and balance. This attitude was instilled in Clark from a young age, keeping her focused and setting a foundation for her future success both on and off the court. "You'll never hear from her parents that, 'Oh, boy, isn't Caitlin Clark the greatest thing in the world?'" Jensen says. "They're continuing to keep her grounded and they're grateful for everything that Caitlin has been able to receive. They don't think they deserve anything. Everything's earned and nothing's promised."[8]

Forward Focus

Without the distraction of dealing with recruiters, Clark could focus on developing as a player. She continued to improve at a rapid pace as she approached high school. She participated in numerous camps and tournaments, constantly seeking to improve her game. Her performances in these settings only reinforced the early impressions of her talent. Coaches like Jensen noted continued improvement in her skills, basketball IQ, and unwavering commitment to practice. Clark's participation in competitive leagues, like the All Iowa Attack, further honed her abilities and exposed her to high-level competition.

As Clark transitioned from middle school to high school, the expectations and attention surrounding her abilities continued to grow. When she started high school, she already had a reputation as a driven and gifted basketball player, and the anticipation of her high school debut was high. With the support and guidance of her family and coaches, she was ready to step to another level in basketball.

CHAPTER TWO

High School Stardom

Caitlin Clark's journey from being a multisport athlete to focusing solely on basketball took place during her high school years. Before high school she had participated in numerous sports. Once she started high school, she decided to concentrate on two sports: soccer and basketball.

She excelled in soccer as a striker, a position that showcased her athleticism and drive. She was often the leading scorer at the high school games. She even collected All-State honors during her first two years on her high school soccer team.

However, basketball was where she truly shone. By her sophomore year, mostly playing point guard, she knew that her future lay in basketball. She decided to concentrate all her efforts on the sport—a decision driven by her natural talent and her ability to dominate on the court.

Major High School Basketball Achievement

Clark's high school years at Dowling Catholic transformed her as a player. While there, she pushed herself to improve her level of play and skills. In fact, her skills were so advanced that, according to her high school coach Kristin Meyer, at times she would get impatient when teammates could not keep up. For instance, if a teammate missed her pass or a planned play fell apart, Clark would sometimes show frustration. She might throw her arms in the air or shout out, and this would make the team nervous, Meyer recalls.

Meyer worked with Clark to help her become more aware of her own behavior and learn how to redirect her frustration or energy into more positive action. One way she did this was to show Clark film after the games so she could see how her body language affected her teammates. This helped Clark learn to manage her visible emotions in order to be a better team player.

With Meyer's guidance, Clark grew as a player and forged bonds with her teammates, leading to their team rising to higher levels. Although Dowling Catholic was not traditionally known as a women's basketball powerhouse, Clark's arrival and play level helped raise the school's profile in the sport. During Clark's years at Dowling Catholic, the team consistently performed well. They reached the Class 5A (the region and division in her state) state tournament her first three years and advanced to the state semifinals in her sophomore year. The team had a winning record each year she played.

As a player, Clark collected an impressive list of accomplishments. One of her achievements as a freshman was that she

In high school, Clark (right) learned how to redirect her on-court frustrations into more positive action. With guidance, Clark grew as a player and forged strong bonds with her teammates.

earned Class 5A All-State third-team accolades from the Iowa Newspaper Association. Then in her sophomore year, she was named to the first-team Class 5A All-State by the Iowa Print Sports Writers Association and the Central Iowa Metro League Player of the Year by the *Des Moines Register*. These awards were just one in a series of honors that highlighted her skill and dedication. She was named Gatorade Iowa Player of the Year twice, an award that recognizes athletic excellence and academic achievement.

Clark's work on the court was unparalleled. Among her many memorable performances, a game during her junior year stands out: she scored 60 points in one game. The team won against Mason City High School, 90–78, with Clark making 13 three-point shots, a state record. "I've seen her get hot before," said Meyer at the time, "but this is just something that's next level."[9]

Not Immune to Challenges

Clark was used to winning, but like any athlete, she experienced disappointment. One of the lessons of her teen years was learning how to deal with life's challenges.

An opportunity for learning that lesson arose during her sophomore year. In 2018 Clark and her father flew to Colorado for the US U-17 World Cup squad try-outs. This team represented the United States in the Under-17 Women's Basketball World Cup, an international basketball competition organized by Fédération Internationale de Basketball (FIBA). A year earlier Clark had made the US U-16 World Cup team, so she figured she would make it again.

But that is not how it played out. She was cut from the twelve-player roster. It was a harsh blow for Clark. "I got the phone call," her father says. "She was crying and just said, 'I got cut.' And it wasn't even the last cut, it was the second-to-last cut!"[10] He met her at the site of the try-outs and let her cry for five minutes. Then Clark's father told her that she needed to now use that disappointment for motivation. As they flew home to Iowa, that is what she decided to do.

In 2018, Clark tried out for the USA U-17 World Cup squad but did not make the cut. Her father helped her direct her overwhelming disappointment into working harder and improving her game.

Recognize How to Improve

Clark put her energy into working harder and improving her game. Even at 6 feet (183 cm) tall, she sometimes had difficulty getting to the rim for a shot when it was defended by taller players. Dickson Jensen, her All Iowa Attack coach, helped Clark realize that she needed to improve her pull-up jump shot, a shot that involves the player, often dribbling toward the basket, suddenly stopping and shooting the ball while jumping in place. This creates space between the shooter and defender. Every day, Clark took hundreds upon hundreds of shots—some closer and some farther from the basket. "That was about the time that she developed her step-back," Jensen says. "She became a much, much better shooter and a deep shooter."[11]

> "That was about the time that she developed her step-back. She became a much, much better shooter and a deep shooter."[11]
>
> —Dickson Jensen, Clark's former coach for the All Iowa Attack

> "A lot of the losses in my career have really fueled me to be who I am today."[12]
>
> —Caitlin Clark

The improvements to her game were evident, particularly in the pull-up jump shot. That shot allowed her to navigate past defenders with greater ease and to score. With Clark, every defeat or stumble pushed her to be better. "A lot of the losses in my career have really fueled me to be who I am today. . . . I'm not sure if I don't have that loss, are we as good?"[12]

All that extra work paid off. The year after she was cut from the US U-17 World Cup team, she and her All Iowa Attack teammates won the 2018 Nike Girls Elite Youth Basketball League national championship. Clark scored 23 points in a 64–61 final, clinching a victory against California Storm (better known as Cal Storm).

Constant Work

Clark identified other weaknesses in her game and devoted herself to improving those areas as well. For instance, she knew she needed strength and endurance to compete at the highest levels. While in high school she developed and maintained an intense training regimen that focused on cardio and strength training. She also took up yoga, with the aim of increasing flexibility and preventing injuries.

Refining her basketball skills was a priority year round. In addition to team practices, she worked on her shooting and dribbling skills on her own. Sometimes she found other people to practice with her, including her brothers and her dad. She also played with Dowling's all-male basketball scout team, which was a practice team used to help the varsity players prepare for games. "I remember specifically I had to guard her," says scout team player Andrew Lentsch. "It was not a lot of fun . . . because you're always worried about either her making a play or even getting embarrassed by her a couple times. I remember one of the first plays of the first practices, she hit a three from deep right in my face."[13]

Mental focus is another cornerstone of Clark's game. She worked on increasing her focus all through high school. Clark taught herself to stay mentally sharp and motivated no matter what occurred during a game. For instance, she learned to deal with hecklers. As a high-scoring player, she was sometimes heckled by the opposing team and their fans. During one game, she recalls, the student section of the opposing team erupted with chants of "OVER-RATED" every time Clark ran down the court. Instead of dampening Clark's spirit, the chants gave her incentive to play even harder. "I kind of let it roll over," Clark said at the time. "Sometimes, you use it for your own motivation."[14] By the time the game ended, Clark had scored 42 points.

She also learned to recognize and appreciate a well-played game, even when it ended in a loss for her team. During her junior year, the Dowling Catholic team faced a heart-wrenching semifinal loss in the Iowa Class 5A state tournament. In that game, Dowling Catholic competed against Southeast Polk High School, a formidable opponent. Despite Clark's 31 points and the team's best efforts, Southeast Polk beat Dowling Catholic 72–61. Clark had poured herself into the season, making this defeat especially hard. Still, she searched for the positive, remarking, "It came down to the end. We made some mistakes. But overall, we played really well, and I'm proud of how we played."[15]

Trash Talk

Trash talking—the act of taunting and insulting opponents on the court or field of play—is common in basketball and other sports. The point of those snide remarks is to distract players from their game, mess with their heads, and disrupt their performance. Some athletes consider trash talking a legitimate tactic. Others view it as poor sportsmanship. Caitlin Clark is not known for being a trash talker, but she learned to respond in-kind while still in high school. When goaded by other players, she would go right back at them. "Just a little bit. She doesn't do it very often," says former high school teammate Josie Filer. "But if you get her going, she'll bark back for sure."

More often, however, Clark would get into the heads of her opponents, not with words, but with her step-back three-pointers, ankle-breaking crossovers, and other moves on the court. "She brought someone to tears one time on the court just by what she was doing, not even what she was saying," Ella McVey, another former high school teammate, recalls.

Quoted in Grace Raymor, "Iowa's Caitlin Clark and the Stories Only Those Who've Known Her Forever Can Tell," *The Athletic*, March 31, 2023. https://theathletic.com.

Playing Style

High school is where Clark established a playing style—smart, aggressive, and precise. It is also where she developed her strengths—accurate shooting and versatility. Whether she drove the ball to the basket, took a midrange jump shot, or sank one of her famous three-pointers, Clark always found a way to shoot and score. And she never hesitated to provide an assist to teammates going for the basket. Her versatility made it possible for her to take on different roles on the court. Whether she was needed to score on her own or to pass and set others up to shoot, Clark could adapt to what the team needed to win.

Even in high school, Clark had the ability to visualize where each player is on the court and, using this knowledge, quickly

Clark has the ability to visualize all players on the court and quickly assess the best route to score. Her high basketball IQ allows her to read the game in ways that others cannot.

Soccer Helped Her Vision

Although Caitlin Clark ended up dropping soccer to focus entirely on basketball, her brief stint with high school soccer held promise for a bright future in the sport. "She was D-I [Division I] material in soccer, easily," her soccer coach, JP Pearson recalls. "She did have a way to go, but if she would have stayed in soccer and made that her No. 1 sport. . . ." Pearson trailed off when speaking, leaving the thought out there as to what Clark could have achieved.

Dickson Jensen, Clark's former All Iowa Attack coach, believes that Clark's brief time playing soccer actually helped develop her court vision in basketball. Soccer fields are much bigger than basketball courts, which means players have to pass the ball to their teammates over longer distances. To do this they have to see more of the field, not just the space where they are at any moment in time. Jensen says Clark's experience with soccer taught her to view the entire court—a skill that has contributed to her exceptional basketball vision and playmaking skills.

Quoted in Chad Leistikow, "Leistikow: Why Iowa Basketball's Caitlin Clark Could Have Been a Superstar in Soccer, Too," *Des Moines (IA) Register*, February 8, 2024. www.hawkcentral.com.

---

assess the best route to score. Her high basketball IQ allowed her to read the game in ways that others could not, and then use her skills to make a play. As an example, during one of her high school games, Clark knew who she needed to get the ball to, but it required that she execute a behind-the-back pass. She had not done that in a game but decided to try it. Dowling scored. At first, her coach thought it was a risky move, but after the behind-the-back pass worked in several games, it became one of Clark's signature moves.

Between natural ability and determined effort, Clark ran up some incredible statistics during her high school years. During her senior year, she averaged 33.4 points, 8.0 rebounds, 4.0 assists, and 2.7 steals per game. Her prowess on the court was undeniable. That same year she was named a McDonald's All-American, an honor reserved for the top high school basketball players nationwide.

Her level of play—even before her freshman year—attracted interest from colleges around the nation. Meyer fielded Division

I college recruiter calls and emails that started the summer before her freshman year. "I had never coached such a high-profile player before," Meyer says. "I started getting phone calls, like, in August before her freshman year, from some top 10 ranked teams, so that was just a little bit eye-opening for me. Especially her freshman and sophomore years, it was non-stop."[16]

All-Around Person

Despite Clark's dedication to basketball, she managed to stay on top of other aspects of her life. By her senior year she had a 3.86 grade point average. She also spent time with friends and family and played with her golden retriever, Bella. During those busy high school years, Clark also did volunteer work—at a food pantry, an animal shelter, the Special Olympics, and a children's hospital.

> "She's very competitive on the court, but off the court, she just loves to have fun and loves life."[17]
>
> —Kristin Meyer, Dowling Catholic High School coach

Clark also found time for a little fun. As her high school coach Meyer recalls, "We had a little free time before a game, and I went to go do some coaching. I come back, and she's doing karaoke on the microphone. And the entire gym was an empty gym besides just her teammates. But that's the type of fun personality she has. She's very competitive on the court, but off the court, she just loves to have fun and loves life."[17]

But when it came down to it, what Clark loved most was playing basketball. And that love was going to lead her to a new, exciting, and challenging path as she followed it toward college play. After being pursued by college recruiters throughout high school, her next step was to decide the best fit for her.

CHAPTER THREE

Transition to College Basketball

As one of the nation's top high school basketball players, there was almost no question that Clark would play for a Division I college program. The question in 2019 was: which one? It was basically her choice, since all of the top women's basketball programs wanted her.

Clark's college recruitment journey started early in her high school career, with the best college programs noticing her exceptional talent as far back as middle school. Her coach and parents fielded interest from schools until her sophomore year, and then she became active in the decision process.

With her family, Clark visited schools all around the country. On the West Coast, they visited the University of Oregon and Oregon State; in the South, they went to the University of Texas and the University of Florida; and on the East Coast, they visited Duke University. Clark also had many options closer to home. These included the University of Iowa, Iowa State University, Drake University, University of Notre Dame, and Creighton University. By her junior year, she had already attracted offers from several schools with established Division I women's basketball programs. Her standout performances with her high school team, particularly her scoring ability and court vision, made her a highly sought-after recruit nationally.

Decision Time

Clark took her time making a decision. While many Division I recruits commit to a team in their junior year (because Division I coaches like to fill their roster as early as possible), Clark waited until the fall of her senior year. She was genuinely torn about her choice. Notre Dame, a Catholic university that also had a rich tradition in women's basketball, heavily pursued her.

Clark initially leaned toward Notre Dame, the reigning NCAA champion at the time, and even verbally committed to them. Her family was thrilled, anticipating becoming dedicated fans and attending the games. "It's a lot of pressure having to choose and decide where you're going to spend four years of your life. We're Catholic and every person, like, idolizes Notre Dame,"[18] Clark said during a 2024 interview. However, as the final decision approached, Clark began to have second thoughts.

The Iowa Hawkeyes recognized early on that Clark had the potential to elevate their basketball program in her position as point guard. Coach Lisa Bluder and her staff were persistent in their pursuit of Clark, stressing how her leadership abilities and on-court potential could propel the team to new heights. They envisioned building a competitive team with Clark as its centerpiece.

> "The coaches are genuine, down-to-earth people. All the girls are really nice and outgoing. That's just the people I want to be around."[19]
>
> —Caitlin Clark

Bluder's approach resonated with Clark, sustaining her interest throughout the process. When Clark visited the University of Iowa, she felt an immediate connection to Coach Bluder and the girls on the team. "The coaches are genuine, down-to-earth people. All the girls are really nice and outgoing. That's just the people I want to be around. You want to surround yourself with people like you,"[19] Clark said a few months after deciding to sign with the Hawkeyes.

The most exciting prospect Bluder presented was the belief that Clark could lead the team to the Final Four of the women's NCAA tournament. The Iowa Hawkeyes had not achieved this

Iowa Hawkeyes coach Lisa Bluder (right) and her staff were persistent in their pursuit of Clark, stressing how her leadership abilities and on-court potential could propel the team to new heights.

milestone since 1993. Clark, always drawn to a challenge, found this goal both ambitious and motivating. "I wanted to go to a program where I could take them back to the Final Four, do something special that maybe hasn't been done in a while,"[20] she said. The idea of representing her home state and leading the Hawkeyes to success deeply resonated with her. Ultimately, she chose the University of Iowa.

Announcing Her Choice

Clark faced a tense moment when it came time to announce her decision. She felt extremely nervous about letting everyone know she had changed her mind. It helped that her parents were supportive. They emphasized the importance of choosing the place that was the best fit for her. Still, she couldn't shake the anxiety of calling Notre Dame coach Muffet McGraw to inform her of the change. Despite her nerves, Clark made the call, confident it was the right choice.

Summer Break?

For Caitlin Clark, the summer after her freshman year at college was far from a break from basketball, but it was an exciting one. She traveled to Hungary to compete in the FIBA U-19 Women's Basketball tournament. Clark and her team emerged victorious, earning her third international gold medal, following her previous wins at the Women's Americas Championship. She was named the tournament's most valuable player, leading her team with averages of 14.3 points, 5.3 rebounds, and 5.6 assists per game. Clark emphasized the significance of team unity, saying, "The chemistry on this team is what made it so fun. The way we move the ball, the way we share the ball, that's what made this so memorable and so special to be a part of. We knew that if our defense was there, we would be unstoppable and everything else flowed from there." Despite not having much of a break that summer, Clark felt it was a summer well spent.

Quoted in FIBA.basketball, "Mission Accomplished: MVP Clark Embraces Leadership Role to Spur USA to More Gold," August 17, 2021. www.fiba.basketball.

To Clark's relief, McGraw was understanding. Then Clark contacted Bluder, who was thrilled to hear that she would be joining Iowa. In November 2019, during her senior year, Clark publicly announced that she would become a Hawkeye when the new school year started in the fall of 2020.

Jumping into Freshman Year

The school year beginning in the fall of 2020 proved to be more challenging than anyone could have anticipated for students all across the nation and around the world. The COVID-19 pandemic emerged in the United States in the spring of 2020, significantly impacting academics, sports, and all other activities at schools and universities. Many academic institutions shifted to online learning. Other activities, including athletics, required masks, social distancing, COVID-19 testing, and quarantining.

Like other college athletic programs, the Hawkeyes women's basketball team faced significant limitations in preparing and practicing for the fall 2020 season. Strict rules dictated what could be done during those all-important summer practices. Clark arrived for summer practice in June. While the team could practice together on the court, to limit person-to-person contact, only the strength and conditioning coach was allowed to be there with the players. The rest of the coaching staff joined the practices in late July but had to wear masks. Players on the sidelines also had to wear masks. Team members or staff who were exposed to COVID-19 or who contracted the infection had to quarantine.

Everyone struggled with the limitations, but the players also tried to keep their mental outlook and physical conditioning sharp. "It's been really good getting into rhythm with everybody and being able to come back,"[21] Clark said at the beginning of her freshman season. Despite the restrictions, she felt the practices helped them bond as a team and get ready for the season.

The team's first game of the season, on November 25, 2020, went well. With Clark as one of the starters, Iowa beat Northern Iowa 96–91. Clark recorded 27 points, 8 rebounds, and 4 assists. Her teammates were not surprised, because they saw the work she put in at practice. "Caitlin's an amazing player, obviously," said then-sophomore and teammate McKenna

> "She works really hard in practice as well—which is something you can't see—and so it's really inspiring."[22]
>
> —McKenna Warnock, Iowa teammate

Warnock. "Everyone can tell that, but she works really hard in practice as well—which is something you can't see—and so it's really inspiring."[22]

Focused Playing

Clark continued to meet and even exceed the expectations of her coaches and team as the season continued. Game after game, she delivered, including a standout performance against the University of Nebraska in February 2021. Clark posted a season high of 39 points, 10 rebounds, and 7 assists in an 88–81 victory, breaking the single-game scoring record at Pinnacle Bank Arena, Nebraska's home stadium. Clark felt that game helped define her direction for her freshman year. "My shot just felt good tonight.

At the end of the game, I kind of knew our offense had become more stagnant, and we needed a big shot," Clark said after the game. "That last 3-pointer, I just kind of pulled up and took it. I knew that I had to. I'm still learning and growing. I think tonight was a big improvement for me knowing what shots to take and what shots not to take."[23]

Clark helped Iowa make big gains in tournament play that first year. Iowa was runner-up at the Big Ten tournament, a collegiate athletic conference with fourteen universities primarily in the Midwest. She was named to the all-tournament team, recording 37

As a freshman, Clark helped Iowa advance to the Sweet 16 of the women's NCAA basketball tournament. Here, she plays against the University of Connecticut, who won the game, knocking Iowa out.

assists—the most ever in the tournament. Iowa also advanced to the Sweet 16 in the Division I women's NCAA basketball tournament, with an 86–72 victory over University of Kentucky, before losing to the University of Connecticut.

Clark also earned honors for own performance. She led the NCAA Division I in scoring that year, averaging 26.6 points per game. She also ranked second in assists, showcasing her versatility and playmaking abilities. Her stellar performance earned her All-American honors and 2021 Big Ten Freshman of the Year. She also became the first freshman to win the Dawn Staley Award, which is given to the best Division I guard. Additionally, she shared the Women's Basketball Coaches Association Freshman of the Year award with friend and former teammate Paige Bueckers. That award is presented annually by Adidas to the most outstanding freshman college basketball player. After that first year, Clark knew she had made the right decision on her choice of schools.

Sophomore Challenges

Clark continued to excel as an athlete in her sophomore year at Iowa, but it was also a time when she recognized areas that needed improvement. The 2021–2022 season was marked by both highs and lows for Clark and her team.

COVID-19 was still raging during that school year. A planned November trip to Mexico for a Thanksgiving basketball tournament was canceled after several players came down with COVID-19. Additionally, they were unable to practice or play any scheduled games for two weeks because of quarantine rules. This disruption significantly hurt their preparation, especially as they faced a major away game in December against Duke University, a formidable opponent.

With only a few practices in the days leading up to the Duke game, Clark and the team felt out of shape. Their lack of practice and diminished fitness were evident during the game. Clark

> "We haven't played in two weeks and a day, missed three games that were supposed to be prepping for this game."[24]
>
> —Lisa Bluder, University of Iowa coach

said she felt off as soon as she stepped onto the court, and the coach noticed it too. "We haven't played in two weeks and a day, missed three games that were supposed to be prepping for this game. . . . But certainly, this was not an Iowa performance that we're proud of,"[24] Bluder said of the game. Clark struggled, missing 12 of her first 14 shots. Her frustration was visible.

It took more practice and conditioning, but Clark and the team gradually regained their form. After getting back into a winning streak, they ended the regular season with a record of 24 wins and 8 losses. That included 14 wins and 4 losses in Big Ten games, which led to them sharing the Big Ten regular season title with Ohio State University.

Relationships Help

What helped Clark improve both her individual performance and her role as a team player were the relationships she built. The Iowa women's basketball team is known as a close-knit group with a strong support system for its players. One of Clark's close friends on the team was standout player Monika Czinano. Their connection showed on the court. "She knows what I'm thinking and she knows I don't have to be looking at her in the eyes to be ready for the ball," Clark said. "I just think we have really good chemistry with one another, and we kind of just know what each other's thinking all the time."[25]

Clark's family also continued to play a significant role in keeping her grounded and focused during the season. Her brothers would often text her before and after games, sometimes with playful jabs if she hadn't performed well, which helped keep her ego in check and fueled her dedication to improving. "They humbled me all the time," she says. "And when I have a game where I don't maybe shoot as good or play as good, like, they're the first to text me to say something funny, but I think it just puts everything into perspective."[26]

One of Clark's closest friends on her college team was standout player Monika Czinano (right). The friends pose for a portrait during Hawkeyes women's basketball media day in 2022.

Academics Too

Having academics to focus on was also crucial in keeping Clark grounded. While basketball was her primary focus at school, she remained committed to her studies. She chose to major in marketing with a minor in communication studies. Her decision was heavily influenced by a lecture from marketing professor Nancy Abram, whose engaging teaching style and insights into the subject deeply resonated with Clark. Clark felt that a marketing major would not only complement her athletic career but also enhance her understanding of how to manage her growing public profile.

The knowledge she gained from her studies helped her navigate her public image and interact more effectively with the media. Clark used her skills to connect with fans on social media, share her journey, and promote her team. "I'm working with executives, accountants and marketers, designers, and getting real-world experience strategically engaging with all these people,"[27] Clark explained. What she learned in school assisted her in handling not just public interaction but also a growing number of sponsorship offers.

Tournament Time

After the regular season, and toward the end of the school year, Clark turned her focus to the Big Ten tournament. The tournament became a showcase for Clark's peak performance. On March 5, 2022, during the tournament semifinals, she delivered an outstanding game, scoring 22 points to lead Iowa to an 83–66 victory over Nebraska. Clark's impressive play, along with her teammates' efforts, clinched the championship against Indiana University, sealing a 74–67 win. The Hawkeyes rushed the court in celebration, and Clark was honored with the tournament's Most Outstanding Player award.

This victory secured the Hawkeyes as a number 2 seed in the NCAA tournament, scheduled to begin on March 16, 2022. Clark was eager to see how far the team could go after their strong season and Big Ten tournament win. However, in the sec-

Quiet Games

During Caitlin Clark's freshman year at Iowa, the COVID-19 pandemic significantly impacted both preseason and the regular basketball season. Clark arrived at college in June for practices, which were adjusted and reduced due to the pandemic. When the season finally started, the game atmosphere was drastically different from what she had experienced in high school. Games were played without an audience, making it challenging without the usual cheers and excitement from fans. However, Clark found a silver lining in this situation. With no one in the stands to watch and critique her, she felt there was less pressure on her performance. As she explains, "We played in front of no one my freshman year but maybe in a way it was a blessing in disguise for me because I got a whole year of college basketball under my belt without all the fans." By her sophomore year, she was ready to embrace the energy from the cheering fans, using their support to fuel her performance.

Quoted in Taco-Bout Network, *Caitlin Clark—Bball Growing Up, Favorite High School Gyms, Recruiting Process, NCAA Tourney Recap*, YouTube, 2023. www.youtube.com/watch?v=lzFC1Flj8pU.

ond round, the team lost to 10th-seed Creighton University. During the game, Clark had struggled with her shooting, scoring a season-low 15 points with 11 assists. The final score: Creighton, 64; Iowa, 62. It was a hard loss. "That was probably the lowest of lows of my career," Clark recalls. "Every athlete has had one of those moments. I had to look in the mirror, and our team had to look in the mirror."[28]

Moving Forward

That loss told Clark that she needed to step up her game. Recognizing her scoring prowess, the other teams had started to ramp up their efforts to defend against her. Determined to make a change before her junior year, Clark decided to focus on building her strength. She understood that increased physical power would enhance her performance on the court and improve her ability to fend off defenders. As the summer before her junior year approached, she committed to pushing her boundaries and elevating her game to the next level.

CHAPTER FOUR

Rising to National Prominence

Clark spent the summer before her junior year improving her physical strength and boosting her shooting accuracy. The summer was packed with demanding workouts and a disciplined fitness routine developed with the help of Iowa's strength and conditioning coach, Lindsay Alexander. Clark's conditioning involved building muscle through a carefully planned diet and a tailored workout program. Her regimen included sprints, squats, jumps, deadlifts, lunges, single-leg work, and ankle stability exercises— all of which were intended to elevate her game.

> "She's made strides over the year, but this is really where she made that biggest jump, because she was able to really dedicate the full summer to training."[29]
>
> —Lindsay Alexander, strength and conditioning coach

With Alexander's guidance, Clark gained 8 pounds (3.6 kg) of muscle. Alexander noted, "This . . . was the first summer where we actually had a full summer of training. And she's made strides over the year, but this is really where she made that biggest jump, because she was able to really dedicate the full summer to training."[29] This muscle gain improved Clark's physical presence on the court and her ability to hold off defenders.

Skills Focus

In addition to strength training, Clark focused on honing specific basketball skills. She intensified her shooting drills, spending hours perfecting her technique. Her routine included 300 shots per session: 100 three-pointers, 100 free throws, and 100 mid-range shots. She also worked on leveraging her legs for more powerful and accurate shots, which was especially beneficial for her three-point shooting.

All the extra work paid off. Clark felt the difference in her performance as soon as the new season got underway. She stated, "I feel like I'm staying on my feet more when I'm finishing around the rim, I'm able to absorb a lot more contact, things like that."[30]

Upping the Energy

By the time the fall semester got underway in August 2022, COVID-19 restrictions had been lifted and support for the team had grown. Fans flocked to the games. Clark's outstanding play

Lindsay Alexander, Hawkeyes' strength and conditioning coach, leads a pregame warmup. Alexander developed a strict fitness plan for Clark.

caught the attention of National Basketball Association (NBA) stars like Kevin Durant, and Iowa's winning record drew large crowds. The increase in attendance added to Clark's intensity on the court. "I get to play in an area full of a lot of little kids, a lot of little girls, that admire our team. A lot of our fans . . . are here at 8:00 pm on a Tuesday night . . . and that's rare for women's basketball, but it's becoming the norm," Clark said at the time. "I'm just really thankful. I'm trying to soak in every second."[31] Attendance at Hawkeye games soared, creating an electric environment in which Clark thrived.

The energy from the fans helped Clark solidify her status as one of the top players in women's college basketball. Despite twisting her ankle in two separate games early in the season, she continued to perform at a high level. The Hawkeyes ended the season with a 31–7 overall record and 15–3 in Big Ten games, finishing second in the Big Ten conference. Then in March 2023, they went on to win the postseason Big Ten tournament. This win earned them a spot in the NCAA tournament. This time Clark was determined not to let the Hawkeyes get ousted early.

This goal was realized when the team advanced to their second Final Four in program history, the first since 1993. Getting

Focus on Mental Health

Caitlin Clark firmly believes in the power of therapy for maintaining mental health. College students in general, and college athletes in particular, would benefit from regular therapy sessions, she says. Throughout college, she found it helpful to work with sports psychologists. They helped her learn to deal with letdowns and successes. Her therapy sessions also helped her find ways to deal with the pressure to perform and the burden of other people's expectations. "It's such a stressful period of your life," she says of being a college athlete. "You're 18 to 22 years old and trying to figure out which way your life's going to go while so many eyeballs are on you, and it can be difficult at times." She found that talking with a therapist helped her deal with the stress and keep everything in perspective.

Quoted in Amanda Lucci, "After the WNBA Draft, Caitlin Clark Says Therapy 'Should Be Normal' for Student-Athletes," *Women's Health*, April 16, 2024. www.womenshealthmag.com.

to the Final Four had been a longtime goal for Clark and a major reason she chose Iowa. She believes her passion helped light a fire in her teammates, and together they pushed each other to be better. "I think my teammates understand I am fiery, I am competitive, and I think that's what they feed off of," Clark said. "They've just had my back through it all. I'm lucky enough to have teammates like that that understand the competitor I am, and I think that's what makes us who we are."[32]

The Final Four

The 2023 Final Four was in Dallas, Texas. Clark recalls Dallas being a whirlwind of events in the days before the first game, with media obligations and open practices where fans could come and watch. Before one of these practices, the Hawkeyes coach advised the team to simply get on the court, do some shooting, and soak up the atmosphere. Then it was time to face the defending national champion, South Carolina.

Clark says the team's mindset going into the semifinals was that they had nothing to lose. Iowa wasn't favored to win, especially since the South Carolina Gamecocks were riding a 42-game winning streak. Clark remembers seeing the Gamecocks take the court on game day (March 31), and noting how tall and athletic they were. But she pushed that thought aside and focused on the game. Iowa then went on to stun South Carolina with a 77–73 victory, earning a spot in their first championship game in program history. "All we did is believe in each other," Clark said. "You know we might not be the tallest, we knew they were going to . . . [have rebounding advantage] but all we had to do is have some heart and some belief and you know we came through when we needed big plays and I'm just so proud of this group."[33]

The joyful celebration continued back at the hotel, which was packed with fans. But time for celebration was short. The championship game was scheduled for April 2, between Iowa and Louisiana State University. The Hawkeyes fought hard but ultimately fell to the Tigers, 102–85. Despite the disappointment, Clark and her team took pride in their achievement and set their sights on trying again in 2024. Their journey also contributed to a historic achievement as viewership for women's college basketball broke records—with Clark playing a central role in this accomplishment.

Major Accolades

Clark's junior year was a season of record-breaking performances. She achieved multiple triple-doubles, a feat in which a player hits double digits in points, rebounds, and assists in a single game. She also reached significant scoring milestones. Notably, during

Clark's junior year was a season of record-breaking performances. She achieved multiple triple-doubles and also reached significant scoring milestones.

the NCAA Tournament, she accomplished the first 40-point triple-double in NCAA Tournament history—men's or women's.

Clark's remarkable achievements were recognized with numerous national player awards. She won the Naismith Women's College Player of the Year, given by the Atlanta Tipoff Club to the top player in NCAA Division I women's basketball each season. And at ESPN's ESPY Awards, an annual event honoring the top athletes and sport performances of the year, Clark was named Best College Athlete in Women's Sports. She was also named Big Ten Player of the Year and earned first-team All-American honors for the second time, among other accolades. These awards highlighted not only her individual talent but also her pivotal role in advancing women's basketball.

Bringing It Together

Clark's goals as she entered her senior year were to finish her college career as a standout individual player and to solidify Iowa as an elite women's basketball program. From the start of the 2023–2024 season, it was clear she was on a mission. The team had lost a key player, Monika Czinano, who had graduated and gone on to play professionally. Clark, known for her behind-the-back, no-look passes to Czinano, had to adapt. She did that and held firm to her belief that she and the returning starters could still lead the team to success.

At the beginning of the season, Clark was the centerpiece of Iowa's homecoming events. She and Iowa wrestling icon Spencer Lee, who graduated in 2021, served as grand marshals for the homecoming parade. Clark also spoke at a homecoming pep rally hosted by ESPN commentator Stephen A. Smith. Smith asked whether she considered herself the best player in women's college basketball. "Yeah, I think any competitor is going to say that," Clark said. "You always believe in yourself. But also, I'm lucky enough to be at school where Coach Bluder . . . lets me thrive, she lets me do what I do best . . . and the rest of the team that I play with, they let me be me too."[34]

Clark also credited her enhanced performance as a senior to improvements in her mental game. Early in her college career, she had struggled with frustration over bad calls and mistakes, but she learned to stay calm and focused. Her teammates believe this development had a significant impact on the team. "She's a fiery, passionate player, which is what we need and what we want on our team. That just elevates everybody else on our team," says Kate Martin, who played with Clark all four years at Iowa. "But for her to be staying so level-headed and so poised . . . I'm really proud of her. Because we need it. When we see that she's calm and not frazzled, then that keeps the rest of us calm, too."[35]

Season Standout

The team's season began with the Crossover at Kinnick, an exhibition match against DePaul University that attracted fifty-five thousand fans and raised $250,000 for the University of Iowa's Stead Family Children's Hospital. Fans continued to come back

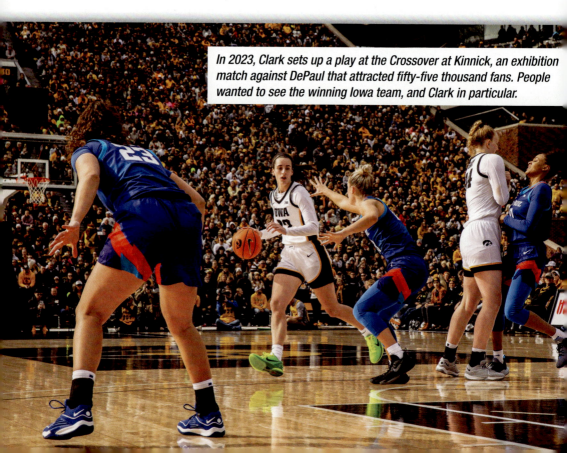

In 2023, Clark sets up a play at the Crossover at Kinnick, an exhibition match against DePaul that attracted fifty-five thousand fans. People wanted to see the winning Iowa team, and Clark in particular.

the rest of the season. People wanted to see the winning Iowa team, and Clark in particular. She did not disappoint. Attendance continued to rise, with all but two games being sellouts.

In December 2023 Clark reached a new milestone by becoming the NCAA women's basketball all-time leading scorer. With 3,528 points, she moved past the previous record of 3,527. Just two minutes and twelve seconds into a game against Michigan, she hit a three-pointer to claim the record. The crowd erupted in cheers. By March she had also become the all-time leading scorer in Division I NCAA men's and women's basketball. While her scoring achievements were historic, analysts also lauded her passing. "Her passing makes her not only the best scorer but also the best all-around offensive player. . . . Clark sees teammates running the floor and often launches a lead pass before they have even turned their heads to know it's coming,"[36] writes Rebecca Lobo, college basketball and WNBA analyst. Lobo also notes that Clark is sixth all-time in assists and praises her for setting up teammates for better scoring opportunities.

Clark's exceptional skills, combined with her teammates' strong performances, led to another stellar season. The Hawkeyes tied for second in the conference behind Ohio State but clinched the Big Ten Tournament for the third consecutive year. This success earned them a spot in the 2024 NCAA Tournament and a place in the Final Four for the second year in a row.

The Final Games

In the NCAA tournament semifinals, the Hawkeyes faced the University of Connecticut Huskies, where Clark played against her former U-19 teammate and friend, Paige Bueckers. The game was tightly contested, with Connecticut's defense proving formidable. However, by the fourth quarter, Clark was making crucial plays, leading the Hawkeyes to a 71–69 victory.

The team then advanced to the NCAA championship game against the South Carolina Gamecocks. ABC reported that the game attracted 18.7 million viewers, an increase of 89 percent

Rivalry

One of the most highly profiled rivalries in women's basketball was that of Louisiana State University star Angel Reese and Caitlin Clark. Reese also received top accolades as a player and had a professional career ahead of her. Their rivalry created drama when they faced each other on the court, to the point of direct confrontation. During the 2023 championship game between their two teams, Reese followed Clark, making a "you can't see me" gesture that implied Clark could not keep up with her. Reese also pointed to her ring finger, referring to the fact that Louisiana would get the championship ring. Reese received much criticism for the gestures, but Clark brushed it off as part of the sport. In fact, Clark had made the same gesture at a previous game and did not face similar criticism. "I don't think Angel should be criticized at all," Clark said. "No matter what way it goes, she should never be criticized for what she did. I competed, she competed. It was a super, super fun game. I think that's what's going to bring more people to our game."

Quoted in Thomas Kika, "Caitlin Clark Breaks Silence on Angel Reese Controversy," *Newsweek*, April 4, 2023. www.newsweek.com.

from the previous year and 285 percent from the 2022 national championship. Clark scored 30 points and gained the title of all-time leading scorer at a women's NCAA Tournament. Despite her impressive performance, the Hawkeyes lost to the Gamecocks, 87–75.

> "I'm sad we lost this game, but I'm also so proud of myself, I'm so proud of my teammates, I'm so proud of this program."[37]
>
> —Caitlin Clark

This game marked the end of Clark's collegiate basketball career. Although she was disappointed by the loss, she took pride in the team's achievements. "Yeah, I'm sad we lost this game, but I'm also so proud of myself, I'm so proud of my teammates, I'm so proud of this program. There's a lot to be proud of,"[37] she said after the game. The audience honored Clark with a twenty-minute standing ovation, recognizing it as her final game. After leading Iowa to two national championship games in a row, the university retired her jersey number, 22.

The accolades poured in. Among them was a message from NBA Hall-of-Famer Magic Johnson. "Caitlin Clark's extraordinary play this season has been the catalyst for growing women's basketball, with record-breaking viewership throughout the tournament," Johnson wrote on X (formerly Twitter). "She deserves her flowers and I want to congratulate her on an incredible collegiate career! (flower emojis)."[38]

> "Caitlin Clark's extraordinary play this season has been the catalyst for growing women's basketball."[38]
>
> —Magic Johnson, Hall-of-Fame NBA player

Finishing Up

While much of her college life focused on basketball, Clark still placed academics high on her agenda. Even with all the time basketball took, Clark graduated with a 3.64 grade point average. However, Clark did not attend her graduation ceremony. Early in the year, she had announced she would be turning pro. This decision brought big changes for Clark at the end of the school year. As the number one pick going into the WNBA draft, the future was full of possibility.

CHAPTER FIVE

Going Pro

Having started college in 2020 during the COVID-19 pandemic, Caitlin Clark had one more year of eligibility to play after her senior year. Clark considered the possibility of going pro or playing another season of college basketball. As much as Coach Lisa Bluder would have loved to have Clark for another season, she wanted Clark to do what was best for her personally. "My role is to point out the opportunities that another year (at Iowa) can provide, the benefits of staying another year,"[39] Bluder explained.

On February 29, 2024, Clark announced her decision. She chose to follow her dream of playing professionally and was immediately projected to be the number one pick in the upcoming WNBA draft.

Draft Day

During the WNBA draft, teams pick new players to join their rosters. The draft has three rounds, and each team gets one pick per round. A lottery system determines the draft order, giving weaker teams first choice for the top players to improve their chances for the next season. In 2024 the Indiana Fever, which finished last among the twelve teams the previous season, had the first pick. The possibility of drafting Clark as a point guard for their team excited everyone at the Indiana Fever. "The night she declared [that she was going pro], somebody texted me and I about fell off my couch, to tell you the truth,"[40] says Fever general manager Lin Dunn.

> "The night she declared [that she was going pro], somebody texted me and I about fell off my couch, to tell you the truth."[40]
>
> —Lin Dunn, Indiana Fever general manager

Draft day was April 15, 2024. Although Clark knew she would be the first pick, it didn't diminish the anticipation. Tickets for the event had sold out within fifteen minutes of going on sale a few months prior, and nearly seventeen thousand people had bought tickets to watch the draft at Indianapolis's Gainbridge Fieldhouse, home arena of the Indiana Fever and the NBA's Indiana Pacers.

Before the draft, Clark relaxed in her hotel room, wearing sweats. Hanging out with her were her boyfriend, Connor Mc-Caffery, a former Iowa basketball player who was on the staff of the NBA's Indiana Pacers, and two of her Iowa teammates, Jada Gyamfi and Gabbie Marshall. Later, Clark changed into a white double-satin Prada skirt and shirt, an embroidered rhinestone mesh top, and black pumps, along with a black leather Galleria handbag. She compared the moment to a prom, something she had never attended due to basketball her junior year and the pandemic during her senior year.

At the event, when the first pick was called, the Indiana Fever selected Clark. "I've dreamed of this moment since I was in second grade," Clark told ESPN after being drafted. "It's taken a lot of hard work, a lot of ups and downs. More than anything, I'm just trying to soak it in."[41]

Joining the Indiana Fever felt like the right next step for Clark. She would still be playing for a midwestern team, close to her family, friends, and boyfriend. Another positive was the opportunity

After being the top draft pick of the Indiana Fever in the 2024 WNBA draft, Clark speaks with the press. She said playing in the WNBA was something she had dreamed of since she was in the second grade.

Saturday Night Live Surprise

Caitlin Clark surprised many with her appearance on *Saturday Night Live* (*SNL*) during the "Weekend Update" segment on April 13, 2024, just days before the WNBA draft. She showed off her sense of humor as she roasted host Michael Che for his past jokes about women's sports. In the segment, Clark made him read jokes she had written for him. She also took the opportunity to thank the players who had forged the way for women's professional basketball. "I'm sure it will be a big first step for me, but it's just one step for the WNBA thanks to all the great players like Sheryl Swoopes, Lisa Leslie, Cynthia Cooper, the great Dawn Staley, and my basketball hero, Maya Moore. These are the women that kicked down the door so I could walk inside." At the end of the show, she stood alongside guest host Ryan Gosling, and other *SNL* cast members then brought her Iowa teammates Jada Gyamfi, Gabbie Marshall, and Kate Martin onstage with her.

Quoted in Brianna Williams, "Caitlin Clark Appears on *Saturday Night Live* Ahead of WNBA Draft," ESPN, April 14, 2024. www.espn.com.

to play alongside Aliyah Boston, who had been the number-one draft pick the previous year. Just as the challenge of elevating Iowa's team had energized Clark, she now had a similar opportunity with the Fever.

Endorsements Too

Product endorsements soon followed. In a typical endorsement agreement, an athlete gets paid by a company to promote its product. As a top college player, she had obtained some endorsements. Prior to turning pro, she had endorsements with companies such as Nike, Hy-Vee (a midwestern supermarket chain), and Gatorade. After she turned pro, more offers started rolling in. For example, Clark became the first female athlete to have her own Wilson Sporting Goods basketball collection. In July 2024 Wilson released the Limitless Series, three balls that were each the color of her high school, college, and pro teams. This was Wilson's first new pro-athlete basketball collection since the 1980s, when it did something similar with Chicago Bulls star Michael Jordan.

Clark also used endorsements to fund the Caitlin Clark Foundation, a nonprofit organization focused on improving the lives of young people and their communities through education, nutrition, and sport. In August 2024, for example, Clark visited her hometown to distribute 350 backpacks to local kids. The backpacks were provided by Nike. Inside the backpacks were notebooks, pens, and pencils supplied by the grocery store chain Hy-Vee and water bottles provided by Gatorade.

Struggling to Start

While working on endorsements and her foundation kept her busy, Clark did not lose sight of her new professional obligations. She had just eight days after her NCAA national championship game to move to Indiana and join practice sessions led by Indiana Fever head coach Christie Sides. On the first day of training camp, Clark played five-on-five, joining center Aliyah Boston, forwards NaLyssa Smith and Katie Lou Samuelson, and guard Erica Wheeler. She immediately had to adapt to a faster-paced game than in college. "And, you know, it's a fast pace, a lot faster than college," Clark said. "You gotta learn quicker, you gotta get your mind fully wherever, you know, there's no time to be tired."[42]

The forty-game regular season began with the Fever playing the Connecticut Sun on May 14, 2024. For the first time in the Sun's history, since their inaugural game in 2003, their season-opening game sold out. Many people attributed this to the "Caitlin Clark Effect," a term used to describe how Clark attracts fans to women's basketball wherever she goes.

While she received cheers for her three-pointers, Clark struggled in her first WNBA regular-season game, and the team lost 92–71. The season continued with Clark facing challenges against strong defenders, and the team had difficulty executing their plays. It was a tough schedule, since their early games were against teams with strong records. After the first eleven games, the Fever's record was 2–9, and Clark had a season-low score of just 3 points in the last of those games.

> **"She's gotta get shots. We've gotta . . . get her open."** [43]
>
> —Christie Sides, Indiana Fever head coach

Sides openly stated that Clark needed to attempt more shots per game after the Indiana Fever lost another game. "She's gotta get shots. We've gotta do a better job of setting her up and setting some really good screens to get her open,"[43] Sides told reporters in June 2024.

In another game, Clark and three other starters were benched in the middle of the third quarter because the coach felt none of them were giving the needed effort. Clark herself acknowledged afterward that she and her teammates needed to bring better energy and improve how they handled their frustration during the game.

It's Not Easy

The transition from college to professional player was not easy, as Clark discovered during the up-and-down start to the season. It felt like everyone was watching. The Fever had drawn about eighty-one thousand fans to their games during the entire 2023 season, but in 2024, after Clark arrived, they exceeded that number in just the first five home games. As for TV viewership, a June 2024 game against the Chicago Sky reached about 3 million viewers, becoming the most-watched WNBA game on any network in twenty-three years. People were tuning in to see Clark.

In addition to the pressure to perform, Clark had to deal with what some considered excessive physical play from other players in the league. In a game against the Chicago Sky, guard Chennedy Carter shoved Clark while she was away from the ball, knocking her to the ground. The play was later ruled an "away from the ball" play and a flagrant 1 violation (a serious personal foul). Clark brushed it off as a heat-of-the-moment play, but similar incidents added to the challenges she faced as a high-profile rookie.

Like many other recent college graduates, Clark was also adjusting to life after college. She had moved to a new city, was living on her own, and was learning her way in a high-profile professional career. There were days when she felt overwhelmed by what was expected of her, and she didn't like letting anyone down.

Clark has spoken openly about dealing with the transition. She says that she is learning to ask for help when she needs it. Whether it's therapy, talking to friends, or taking some time for herself, she tries to be honest about what she needs and lets people know. "I can't accomplish everything in my life. Like, I'm not afraid to ask for help and to tell people, 'Today just is not my day.' And that's okay," Clark says. "Not every day has to be perfect. I'm only 22 years old. I feel younger than that at times. I'm trying to navigate moving to a new city by myself. I'm trying to navigate playing in a new league on top of everything else that has come with it."[44] Clark has accepted that she isn't always going to do everything perfectly and that it's okay to reach out when she needs to.

Clark is fouled during a game between the Chicago Sky and Indiana Fever in June 2024. In the WNBA, Clark has had to deal with what some consider to be excessive physical play from other players.

Finding Her Footing

Getting herself into a more positive state allowed Clark to settle in as the season progressed, and it was evident in her play. The team started to click as well, and together they elevated their level of play. By July 2024 the Fever had worked their way up to the seventh spot out of twelve teams, with a record of 11 wins and 15 losses.

Clark found her footing and established herself not just as one of the best rookies in the WNBA but also as a great player overall. By the middle of her first pro season, Clark had already made history. She reached milestones of 300 career points, 100 rebounds, and 100 assists faster than any other player in WNBA history. She achieved this by her nineteenth game, surpassing the previous record of twenty-two games. In an August 2024 interview, Sides expressed how impressed she was with Clark's strong playing. "It's just been so fun to be out on the court with Caitlin Clark and the things that she sees. Her court vision and the passes that she makes . . . sometimes you just have to pause. I just turn around and am like wow."[45]

Clark was also selected to participate in the annual WNBA All-Star Game. This game is usually an exhibition between the Eastern and Western Conference All-Stars, but in 2024 it was a game between the WNBA All-Star team and Team USA, composed of players selected for the Olympic team. Although Clark was not selected for Team USA, and some wondered about the choice, she didn't express any negativity, saying it left her a goal for 2028.

Clark played alongside Angel Reese, her rival from Louisiana State and now with the Chicago Sky, who was also selected for the All-Star team. The selection is conducted through a combination of voting by fans (50 percent of the vote), current WNBA players (25 percent), and a national panel of sportswriters and broadcasters (25 percent). A sellout crowd watched in Phoenix, Arizona, on July 21, 2024, as the All-Star team beat Team USA, 117–109. Team USA, however, would go on to win the gold medal at the 2024

In 2024, Clark plays on the WNBA All-Star team against Team USA, the US Olympic team.

Paris Olympics. In the game, although she only scored 4 points, Clark had 10 assists, breaking the record for the most assists by a rookie in the All-Star Game. She attributed the win to the team relaxing and just playing the game. "It was kind of just like going out there and playing pickup as a young kid," Clark says. "We didn't have any plays. We didn't have a scouting report. You're just going out there and having fun and playing basketball like you know how to, and I think that's honestly the reason we won."[46]

A Much-Needed Break

After the All-Star Game, Clark, along with the rest of the WNBA players, received several weeks off. Every four years, during the Summer Olympics, the WNBA pauses its schedule to focus on Team USA. For those not on the team, this break serves as a vacation. Clark admitted she was happy not to touch a basketball for a while, since she had been playing constantly for almost a year between college and the WNBA. "There has to be a time where that has to stop, and you have to take care of yourself and

Using Her Name

Caitlin Clark mostly ignores social media and what people are saying about her, preferring to focus instead on her game. However, in the summer of 2024, she felt compelled to address the fact that her name was being used to promote views she did not support. As a high-profile White basketball player, her name was being dragged into culture wars and online debates. Social media posts reacted to the seemingly harsher fouls committed against her in the WNBA and questioned why she was left off the Team USA Olympic basketball team. Some of the comments attributed these actions to her being a White player in a league with a majority of Black players.

Clark initially chose to ignore the social media comments but eventually felt the need to speak out. She was not happy to see that some online commenters were using her name to push claims of racism and misogyny against other WNBA players. Clark stated publicly, "People should not be using my name to push those agendas. It's disappointing, it's not acceptable. . . . Treating every single woman in this league with the same amount of respect, I think, it's just a basic human thing that everybody should do."

Quoted in ESPN, "Caitlin Clark Speaks Out Against Racist, Misogynistic Comments," June 14, 2024. www.espn.com.

do things for yourself," she said. "I think relaxing and reflecting on everything that's happened to me over the course of the last year is going to be super important because my life has moved so fast."[47] Clark used her time to travel with her boyfriend, whom she had been dating for over a year, and some Fever teammates in Mexico, attend a friend's wedding in Iowa, and catch a New York Yankees game.

Once back together for practice in late July 2024, Indiana Fever team members also engaged in bonding activities. Clark and her teammates competed on an Indianapolis ropes course and attended the Indiana State Fair. As the second half of the season was about to begin in August, Clark felt refreshed and ready to put all her effort into improving their team record. The bonding and time off led to a strong start in the second half of the season, with victories over the Phoenix Mercury and Seattle Storm. During the Storm game, Clark set another record—she surpassed the single-season mark for total assists by a rookie, accomplishing this in two fewer games than the previous record holder, Ticha Penicheiro. Penicheiro congratulated Clark on X, encouraging her to keep elevating her game, women's basketball, and the WNBA.

> "One thing at a time. Can't always just be moving on to the next. My focus is right here."[48]
>
> —Caitlin Clark

What's Next?

At just twenty-two, Clark had already accomplished many of the dreams she wrote down as a young girl. But she has many more goals. Helping the Indiana Fever reach the WNBA playoffs, a feat they haven't achieved since 2016, and aiming for gold with Team USA in the 2028 Olympics are among them. While her sights are set high, for now, she's focusing on the task at hand—playing the best she can for her team. "Honestly, I'm just focused on this right now," Clark said. "One thing at a time. Can't always just be moving on to the next. My focus is right here."[48]

SOURCE NOTES

Introduction: Finding Her Path

1. Quoted in ESPN, *Caitlin Clark Tells Her Whole Hoops Story—from Childhood to Iowa to the WNBA Draft*, YouTube, 2024. www.youtube.com/watch?v=N0OZgZpKtog.
2. Quoted in Doug Feinberg, "Caitlin Clark's Childhood Dream of Playing in the WNBA Is Set to Become Reality," Wish TV, April 15, 2024. www.wishtv.com.

Chapter One: Early Years

3. Quoted in Sierra Hoeger, "A CyHawk Sibling Rivalry," *Cedar Rapids (IA) Gazette*, December 23, 2021. www.thegazette.com.
4. Quoted in ESPN, *Caitlin Clark Tells Her Whole Hoops Story—from Childhood to Iowa to the WNBA Draft*.
5. Quoted in IndyStar, *Caitlin Clark's Elementary School Teachers Watched Her Grow Up. "She Wanted to Be the Best, Always."* YouTube, 2024. www.youtube.com/watch?v=yH1VTblfoJQ.
6. Quoted in Chloe Peterson, "We Knew That She Was the Special One: Caitlin Clark Dominating in Her First Season with the Iowa Women's Basketball Team," *Daily Iowan*, March 23, 2021. https://dailyiowan.com.
7. Quoted in Eric Olson, "Caitlin Clark Was a Grade School Phenom: Her 60-Point Game in High School Was a Sign of Things to Come," *Seattle (WA) Times*, February 26, 2024. www.seattletimes.com.
8. Quoted in Stephen Borelli, "Caitlin Clark: Iowa Relatable to Young Fans," *USA Today*, February 6, 2024. www.usatoday.com.

Chapter Two: High School Stardom

9. Quoted in Local 5, *Clark Puts Up 60 Points Monday Against Mason City*, YouTube, 2019. www.youtube.com/watch?v=ithKTmJ-kZg.
10. Quoted in Borelli, "Caitlin Clark."
11. Quoted in Borelli, "Caitlin Clark."
12. Quoted in ESPN, *Caitlin Clark Tells Her Whole Hoops Story—from Childhood to Iowa to the WNBA Draft*.
13. Quoted in Grace Raynor, "Caitlin Clark: Final Four & High School," The Athletic, March 31, 2023. https://theathletic.com.
14. Quoted in John Naughton, "Dowling's Caitlin Clark Seeks Normal Kid Life While Being Sought by College Elite," *Des Moines (IA) Register*, February 19, 2018. www.desmoinesregister.com.
15. Quoted in Matthew Bain, "Iowa Girls State Basketball: Grace Larkins Leads Southeast Polk Past Dowling Catholic's Caitlin

56

Clark," *Des Moines (IA) Register*, February 28, 2019. www.desmoines
register.com.
16. Quoted in Peterson, "We Knew That She Was the Special One."
17. Quoted in Madeline Coggins, "Caitlin Clark's High School Coach
Proud of Iowa Star: WNBA Draft Selection 'Pretty Surreal,'" Fox News,
August 16, 2024. www.foxnews.com.

Chapter Three: Transition to College Basketball

18. Quoted in Brad Crawford, "Caitlin Clark Details Previous Commitment
to Notre Dame & Why She Chose Iowa," 247 Sports, May 13, 2024.
https://247sports.com.
19. Quoted in Adam Hensley, "Caitlin Clark: The Star Player," *Sports Illustrated*, April 21, 2020. www.si.com.
20. Quoted in Peterson, "We Knew That She Was the Special One."
21. Quoted in Chloe Peterson, "Iowa Women's Basketball Team Adapting
to Changes During Voluntary Workouts," *Daily Iowan*, July 1, 2020.
https://dailyiowan.com.
22. Quoted in Dargan Southard, "Iowa Women's Basketball: Caitlin Clark's
Riveting Debut Pushes Hawkeyes Past Northern Iowa," Hawk Central,
November 25, 2020. www.hawkcentral.com.
23. Quoted in Southard, "Iowa Women's Basketball."
24. Quoted in Aaron Beard, "No. 9 Iowa Returns from COVID-19 Pause,
Loses at Duke 79–64," Fox 16, December 3, 2021. www.fox16.com.
25. Quoted in Jack Lido, "Monika Czinano & Caitlin Clark: A Match Made in
Hoops Heaven," KCRG, January 31, 2022. www.kcrg.com.
26. Quoted in Arman Sharma, "They Humble Every Time: Caitlin Clark
Reveals Haters Kept Iowa Star Grounded Since Childhood," Sportskeeda, March 23, 2024. www.sportskeeda.com.
27. Quoted in Joseph Allen, "What Is Caitlin Clark Majoring In?," Distractify, April 5, 2024. www.distractify.com.
28. Quoted in Alexa Philippou and Michael Voepel, "Women's Final Four
2024: Caitlin Clark & Paige Bueckers Showdown," ESPN, April 5,
2024. www.espn.com.

Chapter Four: Rising to National Prominence

29. Quoted in Meredith Cash, "Caitlin Clark Put On 8 Pounds of Muscle to
'Take Her Game to the Next Level.' Here's How She Did It, According
to the Trainer Who Helped Her," Business Insider, March 31, 2023.
www.businessinsider.in.
30. Quoted in Cash, "Caitlin Clark Put On 8 Pounds of Muscle to 'Take Her
Game to the Next Level.'"
31. Quoted in WBB Clips, *Caitlin Clark Talks About the Iowa Crowd During Postgame Sideline Interview*, YouTube, January 3, 2024. www
.youtube.com/watch?v=ozuVAp2bELg.
32. Quoted in Taco-Bout Network, *Caitlin Clark—Bball Growing Up, Favorite High School Gyms, Recruiting Process, NCAA Tourney Recap*,
YouTube, 2023. www.youtube.com/watch?v=lzFC1Flj8pU.

33. Quoted in Homero De la Fuente and Issy Ronald, "Iowa vs. South Carolina: Caitlin Clark in March Madness," CNN, April 1, 2023. www.cnn.com.
34. Quoted in University of Iowa, *Stephen A. Smith Full Interview with Caitlin Clark*, YouTube, October 10, 2023. www.youtube.com/watch?v=PSRXbXGndTE.
35. Quoted in Nancy Armour, "Caitlin Clark Mastered Her Mental Game: That Has Iowa in Title Game," *USA Today*, April 7, 2024. www.usatoday.com.
36. Quoted in Rebecca Lobo, "Caitlin Clark Breaks Scoring Record: Pistol Pete Maravich's Record Falls," ESPN, March 3, 2024. www.espn.com.
37. Quoted in Stan Becton, "What Caitlin Clark Said After Her Last Game: Iowa National Championship Game," NCAA, April 7, 2024. www.ncaa.com.
38. Quoted in Nick Kosko, "Magic Johnson Presents Caitlin Clark with Her Flowers over Career Achievements," MSN, 2024. www.msn.com.

Chapter Five: Going Pro

39. Quoted in Jeff Linder, "Lisa Bluder on Mentoring Caitlin Clark: Her Stay or Go Pro Decision," *Cedar Rapids (IA) Gazette*, December 15, 2023. www.thegazette.com.
40. Quoted in Isabel Gonzalez, "Caitlin Clark Drafted by Fever: Indiana Officially Selects Iowa Legend with No. 1 Pick in 2024 WNBA Draft," CBS Sports, August 17, 2024. www.cbssports.com.
41. Quoted in Gonzalez, "Caitlin Clark Drafted by Fever."
42. Quoted in Chloe Peterson, "Caitlin Clark Keeps Momentum Rolling in Indiana Fever Training Camp," IndyStar, April 28, 2024. www.indystar.com.
43. Quoted in Alex Butler, "Coach Says Caitlin Clark Needs to Shoot More After Fever's 12th Loss," MSN, June 28, 2024. www.msn.com.
44. Quoted in Emily Bicks, "Caitlin Clark's Vulnerable Message on Her Mental Health Turns Heads," MSN, June 17, 2024. www.msn.com.
45. Quoted in Robin Lundberg, "Fever Coach Christie Sides Gives Caitlin Clark Effusive Praise," *Sports Illustrated*, August 13, 2024. www.si.com.
46. Quoted in Nick Schultz, "Caitlin Clark Reflects on First WNBA All-Star Game Win: Olympics, Team USA, 2024 Paris, Indiana Fever," On3, August 3, 2024. www.on3.com.
47. Quoted in Ben Pickman, "Caitlin Clark's Olympic Break: Minutes and Impact," *New York Times*, August 7, 2024. www.nytimes.com.
48. Quoted in Eric Blum, "Caitlin Clark & Angel Reese: League's Megan Rapinoe," *Daily Mail* (London), August 13, 2024. www.dailymail.co.uk.

IMPORTANT EVENTS IN THE LIFE OF CAITLIN CLARK

2002

Caitlin Clark is born on January 22 in West Des Moines, Iowa.

2014

Clark joins the highly competitive girls' All Iowa Attack basketball program.

2018

Clark and her All Iowa Attack teammates win the 2018 Nike Girls Elite Youth Basketball League national championship.

2019

In July, Clark and the US U-19 team win the gold at the 2019 FIBA U-19 Women's Basketball World Cup in Bangkok, Thailand. In November, Clark officially commits to play college basketball for the University of Iowa, choosing the Hawkeyes over several top programs.

2020

On November 25, Caitlin Clark plays in her first game with the Iowa Hawkeyes, scoring 27 points, with a win over the University of Northern Iowa.

2021

Clark is named Big Ten Freshman of the Year and earns first-team All-American honors after a record-setting freshman season.

2022

Clark becomes the first Division I women's basketball player to lead the nation in both points and assists in a season.

2023

In April, Clark leads Iowa to its first NCAA Women's Final Four since 1993. She scores a historic 41 points in a semifinal win against South Carolina, but Iowa loses to Louisiana State University in the finals. In March, Clark wins the Naismith Women's College Player of the Year, awarded to the top player in women's college basketball.

2024

In March, during her final regular season game, Clark becomes the NCAA Division I all-time leading scorer for men and women. In April, Clark is selected as the number-one overall pick in the WNBA draft by the Indiana Fever, fulfilling her childhood dream of playing professionally. In May, Clark graduates from the University of Iowa with a degree in marketing. In May, Clark also makes her WNBA debut with the Indiana Fever in a game against the Connecticut Sun. In July, Clark earns a spot on the WNBA All-Star team. In August, Clark breaks the record for WNBA rookies with the most assists in a single season.

FOR FURTHER RESEARCH

Books

The Athletic, *Caitlin Clark: Raising the Game*. Chicago, IL: Triumph, 2024.

Sports Illustrated Kids, *Big Book of WHO Women in Sports*. New York: Sports Illustrated Books, 2024.

Linda B. Walker, *Caitlin Clark: Kids Inspiring Biography from a Basketball Phenom: The Power of Positivity, Perseverance, and Passion*. New York: Inspire Kids, 2024.

Jim Whiting, *The Story of the Indiana Fever: The WNBA: A History of Women's Hoops*. Mankato, MN: Creative Paperbacks, 2023.

Internet Sources

Sourav Bose, "Fever's Kelsey Mitchell Talks About Playing High-Tempo Basketball with Caitlin Clark," Sports Rush, August 17, 2024. https://thesportsrush.com.

Natasha Dye, "Angel Reese Is Excited to Play with Caitlin Clark in WNBA All-Star Game: 'Hopefully 2028 We'll Be Olympians,'" *People*, July 17, 2024. https://people.com.

Max Escarpio, "Caitlin Clark Made WNBA History in Indiana Fever Debut," Athlon Sports, May 14, 2024. https://athlonsports.com.

Dillon Graff, "Caitlin Clark Breaks WNBA Rookie Assists Record for Indiana Fever: Fans React," MSN, July 14, 2024. www.msn.com.

Kurt Knue, "WNBA's Indiana Fever Says They Have Seen an Enormous Surge in Ticket Sales Following Caitlin Clark's Introduction to Team," WLWT, June 26, 2024. www.wlwt.com.

Paul Pabst, "Caitlin Clark and the 10-Step Sports Phenom Playbook," *GQ*, March 23, 2024. www.gq.com.

Paolo Songco, "Indiana Fever Boldly Reveal the 'Scary Thing' About Caitlin Clark," Athlon Sports, August 14, 2024. https://athlonsports.com.

Michael Voepel, "Caitlin Clark Reflects on Iowa Career: 'Not a Regret in My Mind,'" ESPN, April 7, 2024. www.espn.com.

Websites

Amateur Athletic Union (AAU)
https://aausports.org
The AAU is one of the largest US nonprofit sports organizations. It provides young athletes the opportunity to develop skills and compete at various levels in basketball and other sports. Its website provides information on how teens can get involved in AAU basketball to improve their game and potentially gain exposure for college scholarships.

Billie Jean King Foundation
https://billiejeankingfoundation.org
Founded by tennis legend Billie Jean King, the foundation promotes equality and inclusion, particularly in sports. Its focus is leadership development, advocacy, and education. Every year, the foundation presents the Billie Jean King Youth Leadership Award to young people who use sport to positively affect society. The website provides information about the recipients and their actions.

Caitlin Clark Foundation
https://caitlinclarkfoundation.org
The Caitlin Clark Foundation, established by its namesake, provides resources and opportunities for youth and their communities through education, nutrition, and sports. It aims to help youth develop skills like teamwork and perseverance that are essential for lifelong success.

Girls Basketball Worldwide Foundation (GBWF)
www.girlsbasketballwf.org
The GBWF empowers girls from under-resourced communities through basketball. Its website provides information on their programs, including basketball clinics, tournaments, and camps focused on sports, body image, and nutrition.

Women's National Basketball Association (WNBA)
www.wnba.com
The WNBA is the premier professional women's basketball league in the United States. On the WNBA website, teens can explore teams, player profiles, game highlights, and the latest news about women's professional basketball.

INDEX

Note: Boldface page numbers indicate illustrations.

Alexander, Lindsay, 36, **37**
All Iowa Attack, 11–12
Amateur Athletic Union (AAU), 11, 62

Big Ten tournament, **10**, 34
Billie Jean King Foundation, 62
Bluder, Lisa, 28, 32, 41, 46
  with Clark, **27**
  pursuit of Clark for Hawkeyes, 26–27
Boston, Aliyah, 48
Bueckers, Paige, 31

"Caitlin Clark Effect," 49
Caitlin Clark Foundation, 49, 62
Carter, Chennedy, 50
Clark, Blake (brother), 8, 9, 10
Clark, Brent (father), 8, 11, 18
Clark, Caitlin, **6**
  awards won by, 41
  birth/early childhood of, 8–9
  chooses University of Iowa, 26–27
  competitive drive of, 9–11
  in Crossover at Kinnick match, **42**
  establishes playing style, 22–23
  at FIBA U-19 Women's Basketball tournament, 28
  future goals of, 55
  in game between Chicago Sky and Indiana Fever, **51**
  as high school player, **17**, **22**
  important events in life of, 59–60
  with Jan Jensen **13**
  joins All Iowa Attack, 11–12
  with Lisa Bluder, **27**
  on low point of career, 35
  with Monika Czinano, **33**
  off-court life of, 24

  playing on WNBA All Star team, **53**
  playing with Hawkeyes, **40**
  rivalry with Angel Reese, 44
  role of parents in keeping her grounded, 13–14
  signature moves of, 12
  speaking to press after WNBA draft, **47**
  talent first recognized by coaches/scouts, 12–13
  training regimen of, 20, 36
  on transition from college to professional player, 51
  with trophy for 2023 Big Ten Women's Basketball Tournament, **10**
  in tryout for USA U-17 World Cup squad, **19**
  wins Most Outstanding Player award at Big Ten tournament, 34
  WNBA draft and, 46–48
  in women's NCAA basketball tournament, **30**
  works on mental focus of game, 20–21
  writes list of goals as third grader, 6–7
Clark, Colin (brother), 8, 11
college recruitment, 25
Cooper, Cynthia, 48
court vision, 23
COVID-19 pandemic, 28, 34
Crossover at Kinnick match, 42, **42**
Czinano, Monika, 32, **33**, 41

Des Moines Register (newspaper), 18
Dowling Catholic High School
  Clark's statistics at, 23
  junior year at, 16–17, 18
Dunn, Lin, 46

endorsements, 48–49
ESPY Awards, 41

Faber, Audrey, 14
Faber, Haley, 14
Fédération Internationale de Basketball (FIBA), 18
Filer, Josie, 21

Girls Basketball Worldwide Foundation (GBWF), 62
Gosling, Ryan, 48
Gyamfi, Jada, 48

Jensen, Dickson, 14
  on Clark's soccer experience, 23
  on development of step-back shot, 19
Jensen, Jan, 12, **13**
Johnson, Magic, 45
Jordan, Michael, 48

Lee, Spencer, 41
Lentsch, Andrew, 20
Leslie, Lisa, 48
Louisiana State University Tigers, 39–40

Marshall, Gabbie, 48
Martin, Kate, 42, 48
McCaffery, Connor, 47
McDonald's All-American award, 23
McGraw, Muffet, 27
McVey, Ella, 21
mental health, Clark's focus on, 38
Meyer, Kristin, 16–17, 18, 23–24
Moore, Maya, 48

Naismith Women's College Player of the Year award, 41

Nike Girls Elite Youth Basketball League national championship, 20
Nizzi-Clark, Anne (mother), 7
Nizzi, Bob (grandfather), 8, 11

Pearson, JP, 23
Penicheiro, Ticha, 55
pull-up jump shot, 19, 20

Reese, Angel, 44

Saturday Night Live (TV program), 48
Sides, Christie, 49, 50
Smith, Stephen A., 41
South Carolina Gamecocks, 39
Staley, Dawn, 48
Swoopes, Sheryl, 48

trash talk, 21

Under-17 Women's Basketball World Cup, 18
  Clark in try-out for, **19**
University of Iowa
  Clark's final games at, 43–45
  challenges of sophomore year, 31–32
  Clark chooses, 26–27
  Clark chooses marketing major at, 33–34
  freshman year at, 28–31, 34

volunteer work, 24

Warnock, McKenna, 29
Women's National Basketball Association (WNBA), 7, 62
  draft system of, 46